FARM ANIMALS

FARM ANIMALS

Dorothy Hinshaw Patent

photographs by
William Munoz

HOLIDAY HOUSE/NEW YORK

To the Ray Pat Miller family, whose love of animals is apparent from the moment they welcome you to their farm.

ACKNOWLEDGMENTS

Dr. Dorothy Hinshaw Patent and William Munoz would like to thank the following people for taking time to share their animals and their knowledge with them: Jack Munoz, frontispiece; Grant Myhre, p. 6; George Ruffato, pp. 8, 29, 65; Dee Sindelar, p. 10; Leonard Salomon, p. 11; Nancy Deschamps, pp. 12, 21, 23, 25, 39; Jerry and Billye Roseleip, pp. 13, 18; Tom Kobitisch, p. 15; Bud and Cindy Westphal, p. 17; Ingrid Stevenson, p. 20; Levi Britton, p. 24; John Munoz, p. 26; Gary Simonson, p. 31; Russ Sherman, pp. 32, 34, 36–38; Richard and Shelley Knight, pp. 40, 75; Charles Cook, p. 41; Ron Currie, p. 42; Wojo Munoz, pp. 43, 69; Sandy Munoz, pp. 44, 46; Chester Munoz, pp. 45, 71; The R. Pat Miller family, pp. 47, 55–56, 63; Al Nelson, pp. 49, 51, 53; Jane Spahr, p. 54; Forrest Davis, p. 61; Adam Arvidson, p. 67; Frank Everett, p. 73; Melvin and Helen King, p. 77.

The photo on the frontispiece is of a Hereford with a white face and a dark red body. JACK MUNOZ

Text copyright © 1984 by Dorothy Hinshaw Patent
Illustrations copyright © 1984 by William Munoz
All rights reserved
Printed in the United States of America
First Edition

Library of Congress Cataloging in Publication Data

Patent, Dorothy Hinshaw.
Farm animals.

Includes index.
SUMMARY: Text and photos discuss farm and ranch animals upon which we depend for survival.
1. Domestic animals—Juvenile literature.
[1. Domestic animals] I. Munoz, William, ill. II. Title.
SF75.5.P38   1984   636   83-18628
ISBN 0-8234-0511-7

Contents

1.	At Home on the Farm	7
2.	Animals that Give Milk	12
	Dairy Cattle, Goats	
3.	Meat Animals	27
	Beef Cattle, Pigs, Sheep	
4.	Barnyard Birds	43
	Chickens, Ducks and Geese,	
	Guinea Hens and Turkeys	
5.	Horses as Helpers	59
6.	Other Animal Helpers	68
	Cats, Dogs	
	Index	79

This lamb gets special attention while waiting for its mother to get sheared.

1. At Home on the Farm

Most Americans today live in cities. But more than a million children are growing up on farms and ranches, where our food is grown and raised. The vegetables and fruit we eat and the grain we use to make bread and cereal are cultivated on farms. Cattle ranches raise our beef, and pig farms produce our pork. Farm children get to know animals well, since they play with the animals and help take care of them.

A "farm" is usually a piece of land where grain, fruit, or vegetables are grown or milk cows are raised. It includes a home in which the farmer's family can live and other buildings such as a barn and a henhouse. Farm families often raise animals and grow crops for their own use as well as for food to sell.

A cattle ranch

A "ranch" is usually a bigger place where animals, like cattle or horses, are raised instead of crops. The word *ranch* is more common in the West than in the East. Sometimes, the use of these two words doesn't make much sense. People speak of a "pig farm" but also use the term "apple ranch."

Many different animals live on farms and ranches. These tame creatures, which have been developed as food, friends, and helpers to humans, are called "domesticated animals." They all originated from wild animals that were tamed thousands of years ago. The chicken, for example, was first domesticated in India about four thousand years ago by taming the wild Red Jungle Fowl. From there, chickens spread to Egypt, China, Greece, and Italy. By the time Christ was born, chickens were familiar all over Europe.

Domesticated animals have many uses. Some, like goats and dairy cows, are kept to provide milk for people to drink and for making cheese and butter. Others, such as pigs and beef cattle, are raised for meat. Chickens are kept on many farms so the families can have fresh eggs. Farmers often raise chickens or other birds for their meat, too.

Animals also help with the farm and ranch work. Different breeds of dogs are used to herd or guard cattle and sheep, while horses perform many jobs. Almost all farms and ranches have barn cats that catch the pesky mice living in the barns.

Horses help plow the fields.

Farm families often keep animals as pets, too. Dogs that guard the house may also make playful friends, and a gentle horse is fun for children to ride.

Some farm families keep unusual animals for pets, work, or food. For example, donkeys are friendly and small enough for children to ride, but they are also strong enough to carry heavy loads. Like donkeys, llamas are good pack animals, too, and they are sometimes used to guard sheep.

This mother donkey takes good care of her fuzzy baby.

Some farmers and ranchers raise llamas and sell them as pack animals.

2. Animals that Give Milk

All furry animals (mammals) produce milk for their young to drink. In some countries, people drink milk from camels and sheep. But in America, only cows and goats are used as milk animals.

A baby goat sucks milk from her mother's udder.

Like many family cows, this Brown Swiss is allowed to keep her calf, which will grow up to be a milk cow like her mother.

DAIRY CATTLE

The milk sold in stores comes from cows called dairy cattle, which are kept on dairy farms. Once a year, a dairy cow gives birth to a calf. It has been growing inside its mother's body for nine months. The calf is separated from the mother after a day or two so that people can take milk easily from the cow. Meanwhile, the calf is fed from a bottle or a bucket. The calf drinks milk or a milk replacer for two or three months. When it is only a week old, it begins to eat hay, too. Female dairy calves are kept and raised to replace old cows. Each calf is kept in its own pen at first, but later, the calves are usually kept together.

Most male calves are sold to people who want to raise them for meat. They are often slaughtered young and used for veal. A very few of the best male calves are kept as bulls, which are used for breeding. Dairy bulls can be very mean and difficult to handle. Partly for this reason, bulls are not usually allowed to mate with the cows. Instead, the liquid which contains their sperm is collected from them, frozen, and sent to dairy farms when it is time to breed a cow. The sperm are thawed out and placed in the vagina of a cow by the farmer. That way, a dairy farmer can choose different bulls as the fathers for his herd.

After having a calf, the cow gives lots of milk, usually about six gallons a day, for many months. Dairy cattle have to eat plenty of food to make that much milk. Twenty pounds of grain and thirty pounds of hay is a normal amount of daily food for a dairy cow. Some dairies keep the cows indoors all the time, while others let them graze in the pasture during the warmer months. On dairy farms, machines are used for milking, and the cows are milked two or three times a day. But many family farms have one or two dairy cows which give milk for the family. These cows are milked by hand each morning and afternoon.

The warm milk from the cow's udder squirts into the waiting bucket.

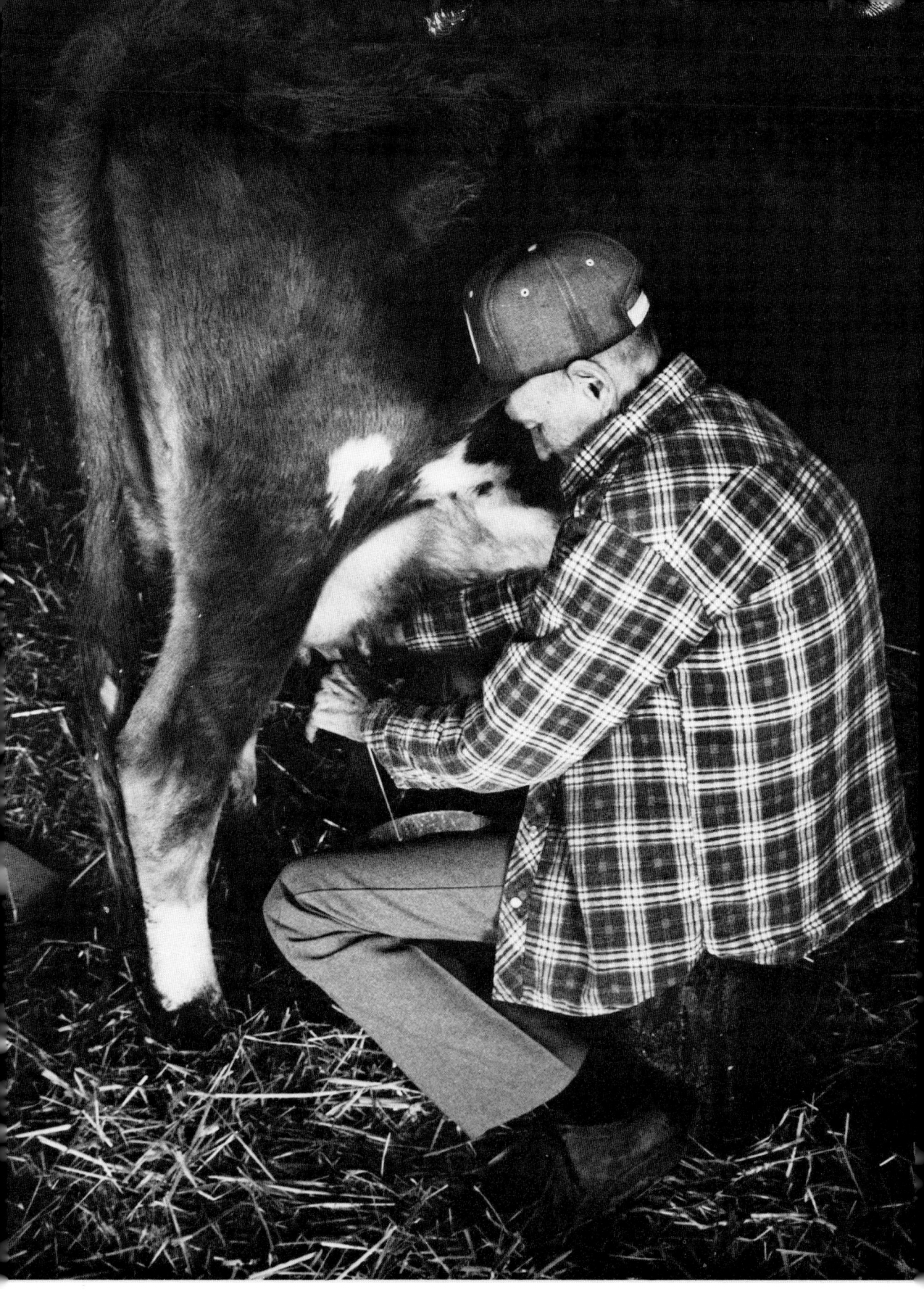

The milk is stored in the udder under the cow's belly. It comes out through four "spigots," called teats. The milker pulls on two teats at a time, one with each hand. As he pulls, he gently squeezes the teat from top to bottom, which brings the milk out. His hands are doing just what a calf does when it nurses from its mother.

Many different kinds of cows are used for milk. Dairies usually have all or mostly Holstein cows. Holsteins originated in Holland. They are black and white (occasionally red and white) and are the biggest dairy cows. Holsteins give more milk than other breeds. A Holstein can produce as much as twelve gallons of milk in one day.

The Jersey cow is especially popular on family farms, since it is the smallest dairy cow. It eats less and gives less milk than the larger breeds do, about five gallons a day. Jerseys are very efficient at converting their food into milk, and they do better in hot climates than most dairy breeds. Jerseys grow up more quickly and live longer than other kinds of dairy cattle. Jerseys originated on the English island of Jersey. They are fawn colored, sometimes with white markings. Their faces have a more delicate shape than those of Holsteins.

These Holsteins produce lots of milk.

Other popular dairy cattle are the Guernsey, Ayrshire, and Brown Swiss. These breeds are in between the Holstein and Jersey in size.

Two Brown Swiss cows

The amount of milk a dairy cow gives is not the only important thing about it; the richness of the milk matters, too. Richer milk has more cream. It contains the fat part of milk from which we get whipping cream and butter. Rich milk is also best for making cheese. Holstein milk is not as rich as that of other dairy breeds. Because it has less cream, Holstein milk is paler than other milk. For these reasons, many dairies have mostly Holsteins but mix in a few other breeds besides Holsteins. When milk from other breeds is added to the Holstein milk, the milk that's sold is more golden in color.

Jerseys give the richest milk; it is sometimes one third cream. Because of this rich milk, candy companies use Jersey milk for making creamy candy such as caramels. The milk from Guernseys is also very rich and especially golden in color, so butter from Guernsey milk is a lovely bright yellow.

GOATS

The goat was one of the first animals to be tamed by humans. Goats have been raised for their milk for thousands of years. Goat milk is easy to digest, so it is often recommended for people with stomach trouble. Some people are allergic to cow's milk, but they can drink goat's milk instead. Cow's milk will separate into milk and cream. But the fat globules in goat's milk are very small and do not separate; the milk is naturally homogenized.

Because they are small, goats make good dairy animals for a family farm. The many gallons of milk a cow gives each day may be hard for a family to use up, while a goat usually produces two or three quarts a day. Goats can live on much poorer land than cows, too, and they need less feed than cattle because of their smaller size. Goats eat a variety of food, including the tender tips of tree branches, but they do not eat tin cans, as some people think.

This Nubian goat makes a good dairy animal for a family farm.

Flower is a half-Nubian, half-Alpine kid.

Baby goats are called kids. While cows almost always have only one calf, female goats, called nannies, often have two or even three kids at a time. Many farmers take the kids away from the nanny while they are very young, but kids are sometimes allowed to stay with the mother and nurse from her udder, too. Most goats are born with tiny bumps on their heads which will develop into horns. These bumps are usually removed during the first days of the goat's life so the animal won't grow horns which could hurt people or other goats. When the kids are about a week old, they begin to nibble on grass, and by the time they are two or three months old, they do not need milk any more but can be fed grass, grain, and hay. Meanwhile, the nanny can be milked for several more months.

Goats are very curious animals. They like to know what is going on and will follow people to see what they are doing. They also climb well and can sometimes crawl under fences. Farmers with goats have to be careful, or their animals can escape and eat up the garden vegetables or chew away the branches of precious fruit trees. The kids are very playful. They romp and jump around together, sometimes leaping straight up in the air with all four delicate hooves off the ground at one time. Kids are also friendly. A young kid will come to a person, just like a puppy does, to be petted.

Male goats, or "billies," are bigger than nannies. Most farms do not keep billy goats around, since they smell bad during the breeding season. Like cows, goats can be bred artificially.

Flower plays hide-and-seek with the photographer.

Some dairy goats, such as the Alpine, are from Europe. They have straight faces and pricked-up ears. In the wintertime, these goats grow thick, protective coats.

This pygmy goat has the straight face of a European goat.

The face of a Nubian goat is rounded, and its ears are long.

Another kind of dairy goat, the Nubian goat, comes from Africa. It has long, hanging, silky ears, and its coat is short and glossy. The Nubian goat has a "Roman nose"—it is rounded outwards instead of straight.

The Angora goat, which comes from Asia Minor, is raised for its long, silky, white fur, called mohair. Every six months, Angoras are shorn of their coats. The shiny mohair is usually mixed with other fibers, adding softness and shininess to the resulting fabric.

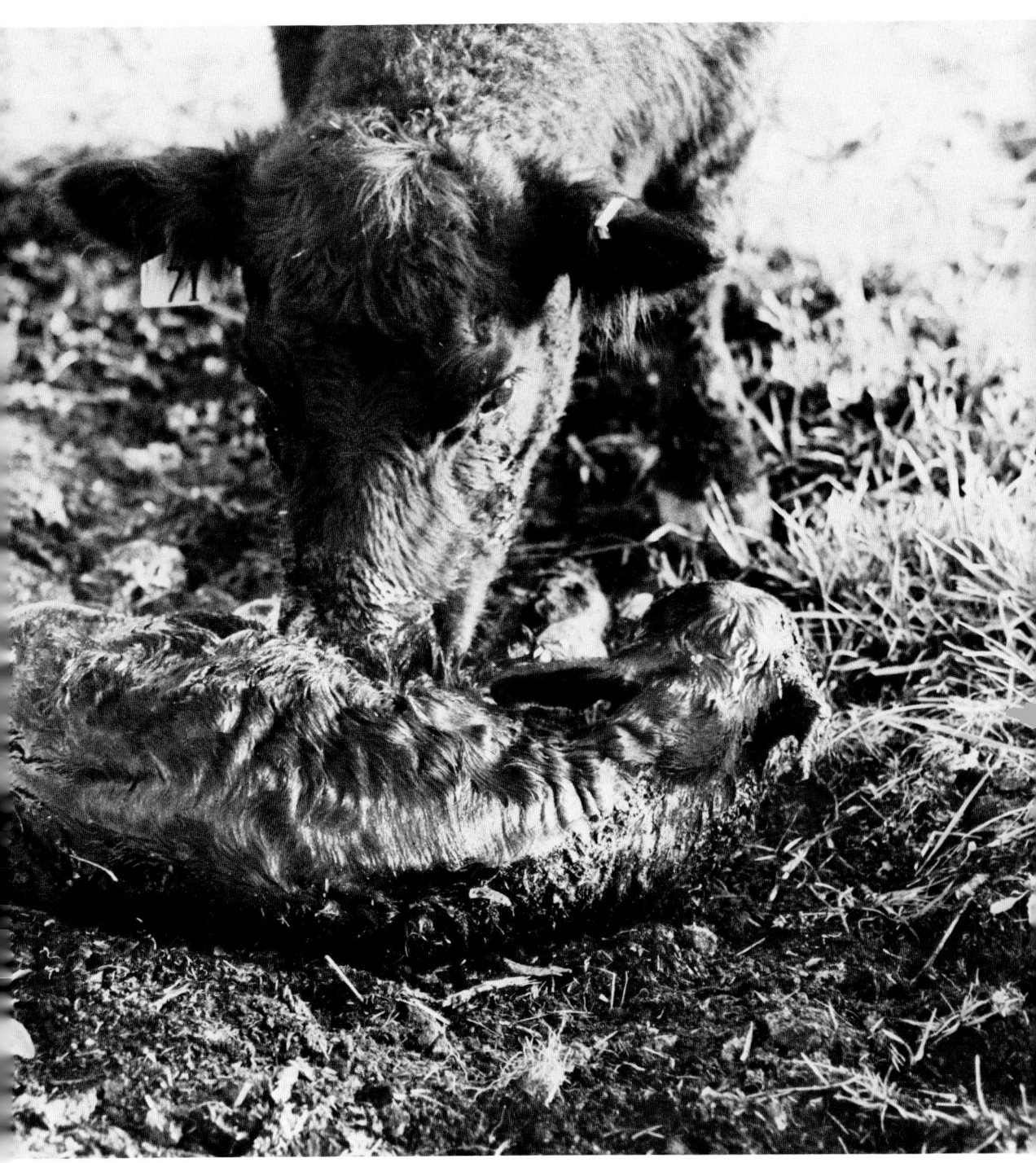
This Angus cow gently noses her newborn calf.

3. Meat Animals

Farmers and ranchers often make a living raising animals for meat. Cattle (for beef), pigs (for pork), and sheep (for lamb) are all popular meat animals in America.

BEEF CATTLE

Beef cattle are different from dairy cattle. Dairy breeds were developed to produce plenty of milk, but beef cattle must grow fast and put on a lot of muscle, which is the meat we eat. While dairy cattle look lean and a bit bony, beef cattle are muscular and sturdy and often have short legs.

Beef cattle live outdoors all their lives. They are usually born in late winter or in the springtime. The rancher keeps a close watch on his animals during calving and helps cows that have difficulty giving birth. But after the calves are born, most of them are left in the pasture with their mothers until they are two or three months old. Then they are branded.

At branding time, the cattle are rounded up and herded into corrals. The calves are separated from their mothers. One at a time, the calves are branded. Each ranch has its own unique branding mark, which is burned into the skin of the calf by a hot iron. Once a calf is branded, everyone can see to whom it belongs, even if it strays. In addition to being branded, each calf is given a shot to protect it from disease. The male calves are also castrated. Their male sex glands, called the testes, are removed. Castrated cattle are called steers. While bulls will fight with one another, steers are much gentler and can be kept together easily.

After branding, the cattle are released again into the pasture. The calves grow and, bit by bit, eat more grass and spend less time with their mothers. When the calves are about six months old, they are separated from their mothers. The calves and cows moo for one another for a few days, but soon they are used to being apart. The best young cows, called heifers, are kept to replace old cows. The rest of the heifers are either sold to other ranchers or, along with the steers, are used for meat.

Some ranchers sell their young steers in the fall, but when there is enough hay to feed them, the steers are kept through the winter. In the springtime, grass grows again, and the rancher can leave his steers on the range until fall. Then, when they are about a year-and-a-half old and weigh about one thousand pounds, he sells the steers to a feedlot operator. The steers are shipped to a feedlot, where they are kept in corrals and fed rich grain. The grain feeding results in beef with lots of fat or "marbling" in the meat. The more marbling, the more tender the meat, and the higher price it brings.

The most popular beef cattle in America are the Hereford and the Angus. Both of these breeds came originally from Great Britain. They are smaller than some other kinds of cattle but do well on the wide open plains of the Western states. Herefords have a thick red-and-white coat and white faces. They are usually calm animals, and they survive well on poor land. Angus are usually pure black, but there is also a Red Angus breed. Angus cows are especially fine mothers and take good care of their calves. Angus meat is so good that some restaurants specialize in serving meat only from this breed.

These Herefords have both brands and ear tags to identify them.

Other beef breeds are also raised in the United States. The white Charolais, from France, are larger than Herefords and Angus. The Charolais cow produces plenty of rich milk, and Charolais calves grow very quickly. Other European breeds, such as the Simmenthal, from Switzerland, and the Limousin, from France, are becoming more popular, too. These are big cattle which produce plenty of meat. The Shorthorn, from Great Britain, makes so much milk that it is sometimes raised as both a beef and a milk cow. In Texas, Shorthorns have been crossed with Brahmans, resulting in a new breed called the Santa Gertrudis. Brahmans come from India, where it is very hot, and the Santa Gertrudis has inherited the heat tolerance of the Brahman. The old-fashioned Longhorn, a hardy breed raised in the Old West, is again becoming popular. Longhorns produce small calves. For this reason, Longhorn bulls are sometimes used to mate with heifers of other breeds. Heifers are smaller than full-grown cows and sometimes have trouble giving birth to big calves. It is easier for them to have the smaller, half-Longhorn calves.

Cattle ranchers often use other crosses, too. For example, a Charolais bull may be bred to Angus cows. The resulting calves are a peculiar smoky color. They grow faster than a purebred Angus calf would.

The Charolais is a breed which is becoming more popular in the United States.

Pigs eat different foods, including these discarded potatoes.

PIGS

Pigs are thought by many people to be the smartest animals on the farm. When given lots of attention, a pig can become as rewarding a pet as a dog. It can learn to come when called, to roll over, and to retrieve. Pigs can be taught to use their sense of smell to zero in on things people want but can't easily locate. In France, pigs are trained to dig up the rare and expensive truffle, a fungus which lives underground. They have also been used during wartime to sniff out land mines.

Pigs are more than twice as efficient as cattle at turning feed into meat. Pigs will eat a variety of foods and grow very fast. Their rapid growth and varied diet make pigs a good choice for family meat animals. Pigs can be fed corncobs, stale bread, and other leftovers from the table in addition to pig feed bought at a store.

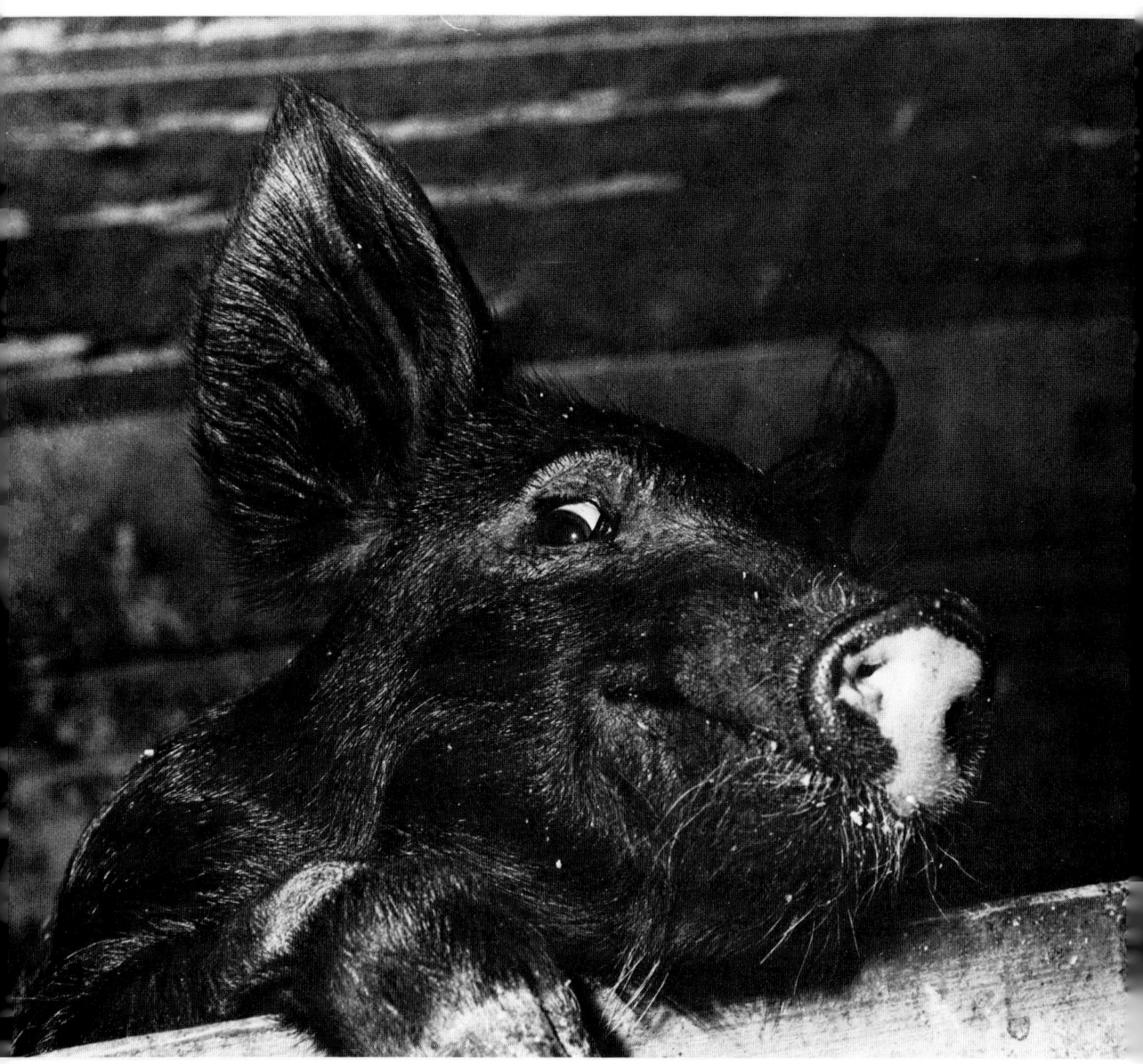
A piglet

While some pigs today live on family farms, most pigs grown for pork sold in stores are raised on big farms which specialize in pork. The male pigs, or boars, and the female pigs, or sows, may be kept outside. But from the time the piglets are born, those being raised for market are kept in indoor pens.

When the sow is ready to give birth, she is brought into a building and placed in a small pen. The eight to fourteen piglets are born one at a time and quickly become active. They can walk around within a few minutes of birth and soon find the double row of teats on their mother's belly. At first, their only food is milk, and the piglets grow amazingly fast. At birth, each weighs only two or three pounds, but within a week, it doubles in size. By three weeks of age, many young pigs have reached fifteen pounds in weight.

When the piglets are four weeks old, their mother is put back outside, and they are kept in big groups indoors. There, they feed on a carefully mixed food made largely from cornmeal and soybean meal. When the pigs reach two hundred twenty pounds, most of them are sent to market and sold. A few of the best may be picked out and kept to replace old sows and boars.

Pigs for market are usually raised indoors.

There are more than three hundred breeds of pigs in the world, but crossbreeds are often raised for pork. Three different breeds may be used in a cross. For example, Hampshire pigs, which are meaty, are crossed with Yorkshire pigs, which are good mothers, and with Duroc hogs, which grow fast and are hardy. By using combinations like this, pig farmers hope to get the good qualities of different breeds into one animal.

Pigs enjoy mud baths on a hot day. Since they cannot sweat, pigs must cool their bodies by wetting them on the outside with water or mud. The pig in front has the banded pattern of a Hampshire hog.

Farmers used to say that everything from the pig except the squeal was used. This is even more true today. Not only is the skin used for leather and the fat for lard, but the valves from pig's hearts are carefully cut out and used to replace damaged human heart valves. Pigskin can also be especially treated and used to cover severe burns while new skin is growing back.

This pig is taking a sunbath on a pig farm.

SHEEP

Sheep are very useful farm animals. The meat from young animals—about six months old—is tasty lamb. And the wool from sheep makes fine clothing. Sheep, like goats, can do better on poor pasture than cattle.

There are more than a billion sheep in the world, representing over eight hundred breeds. Several common sheep breeds on American farms and ranches, such as the Southdown, are white all over. But perhaps the most familiar kind in America is the Suffolk. These sheep have black faces and legs, with white wool. Like cattle and pigs, sheep are often crossbred to get the good traits of more than one breed.

This Suffolk ewe has been eating hay, bits of which cling to her.

Lambs are usually born in the springtime, although in some mild climates, sheep also give birth in the fall. The female sheep, called a ewe, often has twins or even triplets. Feeding three babies is too much for a ewe, so when she has triplets, one of the lambs must be fed and cared for in another way. Sometimes a ewe with only one lamb, or a ewe whose lamb has died, can be persuaded to take on the extra lamb. If no substitute mother can be found, the farmer must feed the lamb from a bottle until it is old enough to live on grass and grain.

Three young lambs

This part-Columbia sheep's wool is thick before shearing.

The ewes and lambs live in the pasture, where the lambs enjoy romping and playing together. They run and jump and climb on hay bales and in piles of manure. Since the ewes wean their lambs, gradually preventing them from getting milk, the babies and mothers do not need to be separated like beef cattle.

In the spring, the sheep are sheared. Some ranchers have their sheep sheared before the lambs are born, but others wait until afterwards. When the sheep is sheared, electric clippers are used to shave the wool—called the fleece—close to the skin. A sheared sheep looks only half as big as an unsheared one! The wool is rolled up and then packed into big bags and taken to market.

The shearer must support the sheep's body with one hand while he shears with the other.

This mother hen watches carefully over her chicks.

4. Barnyard Birds

Chickens, ducks, geese, and other birds are often raised by farm families for meat or eggs. Birds do not take up a lot of room, and store-bought eggs just can't compare with farm-fresh ones. The word "poultry" is used in general for barnyard birds, although in the grocery store, poultry usually means just chicken and turkey.

Some chickens, like this one, will sit on their eggs and take care of them.

CHICKENS

Most birds will attack you if you try to take away their eggs from the nest. But chickens bred as egg layers will only sometimes peck at a human hand as it slips under a hen to collect newly laid eggs. As a matter of fact, many egg layers will not even sit on their eggs. Chickens which lay the eggs sold in stores couldn't sit on their eggs if they wanted to. These animals are kept in row upon row of small cages indoors, and their eggs roll away to collection sites as soon as they are laid.

A hen usually lays from sixty to one hundred twenty eggs a year, although some hens have been known to produce two hundred fifty eggs in one year. The farmer needs to collect the eggs at least once a day, or they will get stale. Not all chicken eggs are white. Many chickens lay brown eggs, and one breed, the Araucana from Chile, lays greenish blue "Easter eggs."

A nest of chicken eggs

If the farmer wants to raise chicks instead of collecting eggs, he needs to find a hen that will sit on a nest of eggs and brood them for three weeks. One hen can cover from nine to fifteen eggs in her nest. She must keep them warm and turn them over every day so that the chick develops correctly and doesn't stick to the shell. Once the chicks hatch, the hen takes care of them. She leads them around the barnyard and helps them find food by scratching in the dirt.

If the farmer can't find a "broody hen," he can put the eggs in a warm incubator to hatch. Then he must turn them each day himself.

After chicks hatch, they still return to the safety of their mother when frightened.

A rooster

The male chicken is called a rooster. Hens will lay eggs for market even without mating with a rooster. But if the farmer wants to raise chicks, he needs to have a rooster. One rooster will mate with many hens. Roosters are famous for crowing at dawn, but they crow at other times of day, too. Roosters have growths of red flesh on their heads. The one on top is called the "comb," and the two which hang down below the beak are the "wattles." Roosters also have long, pretty feathers. They develop sharp spurs on their legs for fighting with other roosters.

Chickens raised for meat are different from those kept for eggs. Instead of being selected for the number and size of eggs they lay, these breeds are chosen for fast growth and meaty bodies. While egg layers are often lively birds, fryer chickens are quiet. They spend most of their time eating and resting, so they grow quickly.

This is a Muscovy duck. Muscovies don't quack. They hiss like geese instead.

DUCKS AND GEESE

Ducks and geese are popular with farmers, too. They are called "waterfowl," since their wild ancestors were water birds. In nature, ducks mate in the water, and a heavy male may have trouble mating on land. Even so, a farmer can raise waterfowl without a pond, although the birds do enjoy a dip if they have a place to swim. In some Asian countries, ducks are raised in the watery rice paddies, where they pull out the weeds.

Ducks are valued mainly for their meat. In just two months, a duckling can grow into a fat roasting bird weighing five pounds after cleaning. Ducks also lay big eggs, which taste stronger than chicken eggs. The most popular ducks are big white ones called Pekin ducks, which were brought from China a long time ago. Pekin ducks have bright orange-yellow bills and orange legs. Their wings are short, so they can't fly far. All Pekin ducks look alike, which makes it difficult to identify which are males and which are females before they are old enough to mate. Another popular duck is the Rouen, or Domesticated Mallard. This duck looks like the wild Mallard duck, but is almost three times as big. The male Rouen has a beautiful, glossy green head with a white ring around his neck. His breast is a rich, reddish brown, and his tail is white. The female Rouen is plainly colored, with streaked brown feathers. Both males and females have a metallic, violet-blue patch on each wing, with a narrow border of white on each side.

These are Rouen, or Domesticated Mallard, ducks. The colorful male is on the right, while the plainer female is on the left.

Ducks are usually kept in flocks, with one male, or drake, to every six or so females, called ducks. In the springtime, the ducks begin to lay eggs, about one every day until each has laid as many as two hundred. The farmer usually collects the eggs as they are laid and hatches them in an incubator, since most domesticated ducks are not very good mothers. They lay the eggs here and there, filling several nests but never settling down to sit long enough on the eggs for them to hatch.

With no mother to take care of them, the ducklings must be kept indoors in a warm place for three or four weeks, until they are big enough to live outside at air temperatures. The ducklings are fed cornmeal or a feed made from mixed grain.

Geese are good for more than their tasty meat. They provide fine, soft feathers used in making high quality pillows, quilts, and warm jackets. Geese are often allowed to roam about the farm, since they eat weeds and pests and actually make good guard animals. A full-grown gander, or male goose, may weigh more than thirty pounds and his beak is strong enough to break a man's arm! A goose will threaten any intruder, whether it is a human or an animal, by spreading out its wings and hissing. If the foolish trespasser doesn't leave, the goose will attack, biting and beating with its wings.

These geese are warning the photographer to keep his distance.
The one behind, with the knob on his head, is an African.
The female is a crossbreed.

Geese live in pairs and, unlike domesticated ducks, take good care of their babies, called goslings. Both the parents co-operate in caring for the six or more goslings, bravely defending them against any danger. Geese are easy to feed and care for, too. They are best off when left to forage for food on their own, grazing and weeding most of the time, with only a little grain provided each day.

Geese mate for life. Here are two pairs of geese. The white ones are Embens, while the other pair are Toulouse.

These Guinea Hens are feeding in an old cornfield.

GUINEA HENS AND TURKEYS

Guinea hens and turkeys are birds raised on farms for their meat. Guinea hens are often allowed the run of the barnyard, where they find insects and weeds to eat. Guinea hens grow more slowly than chickens; at seven months of age, they are slaughtered and are about the same size as a frying chicken. The guinea hen provides juicy, flavorful dark meat. Guinea hens mate in pairs, and the male helps take care of the dozen or more young. Because guinea hens can be left pretty much alone, they are becoming more and more popular on family farms.

Turkeys are native to Central and North America. The early explorers, such as Cortes, were amazed to see the Aztecs tending flocks containing countless thousands of turkeys. Unlike European and Asian civilizations, the Central American peoples had not domesticated large meat animals, and turkeys and dogs were the only tame creatures they grew for food.

Young turkeys

The modern domesticated turkey is very different from its wild ancestors. Turkeys have been bred for broad, thick breasts for many generations. The result is a heavy, awkward bird which has trouble walking if allowed to get very big. It cannot fly, and usually cannot mate successfully. For this reason, turkeys are usually bred artificially. Tame turkeys grow quickly and can reach seventy pounds in weight. There are two major kinds of domesticated turkeys, the white and the bronze. The bronze looks like a big version of the wild turkey.

Today, as in the past, turkeys are often raised in big flocks. When the flock is disturbed, an alarmed "gobble" sound passes through the flock like the ripples of water from a stone thrown into a pond. While wild turkeys are smart, domesticated turkeys are quite stupid. This has resulted in the familiar use of the word "turkey" as an insult.

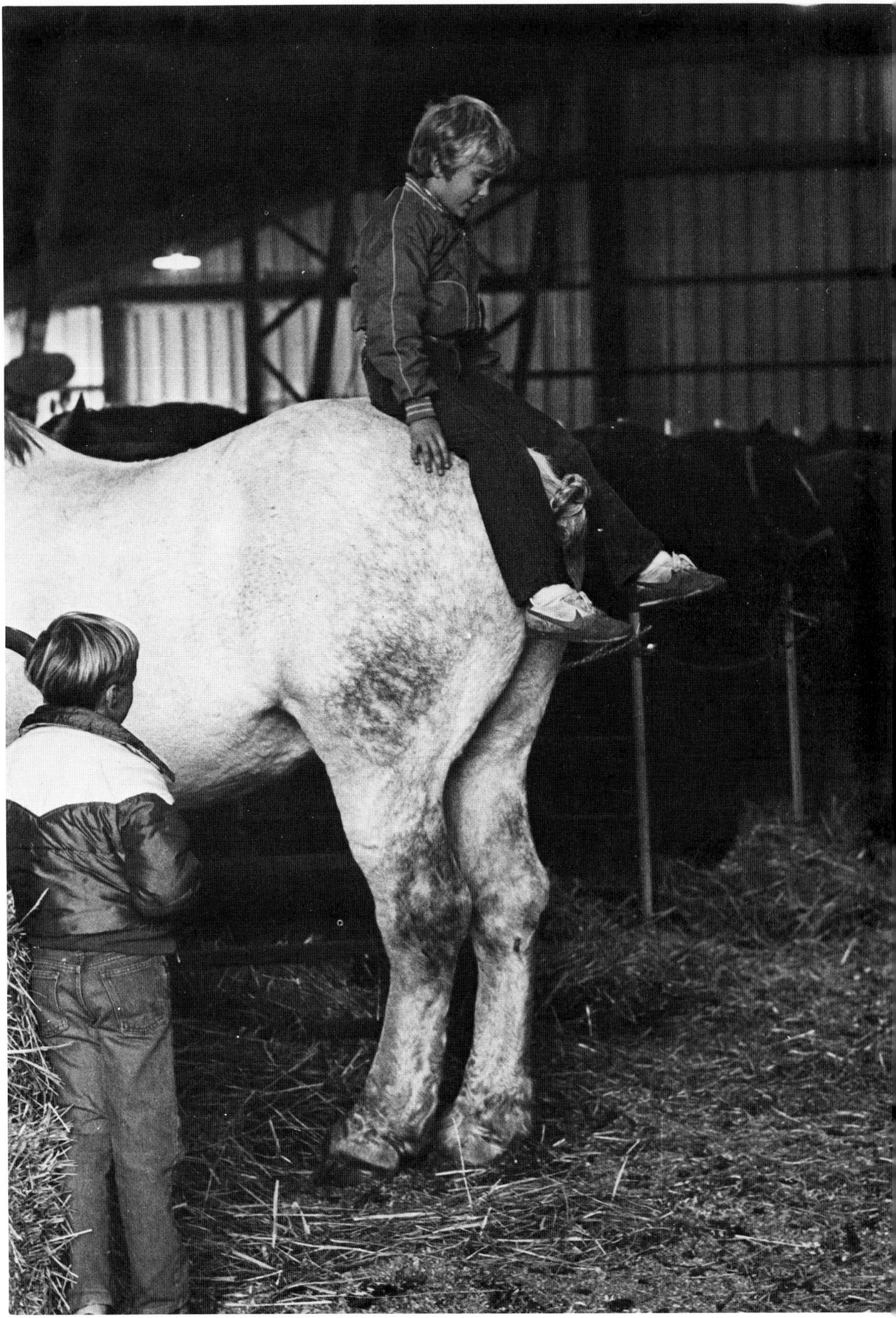

5. Horses as Helpers

Horses perform many jobs on farms and ranches. Before the tractor was invented, farms couldn't survive without animals such as workhorses or oxen. In America, most farmers used horses for plowing and harvesting, and they pulled wagons with heavy loads. When the tractor came along, many farmers got rid of their horses. They did their plowing with tractors and bought expensive machinery to do other farm work. But today, the price of machinery is so high and fuel is so expensive that many farmers are returning to using horses.

Horses have several advantages over tractors. For one thing, they are quieter! For another, a horse-drawn hay cutter can get closer to irrigation ditches and work uneven ground more easily than one pulled by a tractor. Besides, the hay and grain a horse eats are a lot cheaper than the gasoline needed by a tractor. Workhorses can also reproduce themselves, and a female horse, or mare, can be worked until just before she has her baby, called a foal.

While this Percheron horse waits its turn at a fair, it patiently allows a boy to use its rear end as a slide.

Strong, gentle breeds of horses are usually used for farm work. These big animals are called "draft horses." Clydesdales, from Scotland, have brown or black bodies and white legs with long hair on them. Clydesdales pick their feet up high when they move. Percherons, which originally came from France, are born black, but some turn gray as they grow older. Percherons are especially beautiful draft horses. Belgian horses come in many colors. Most Belgians in America, however, have red-brown or tan bodies and lighter manes and tails. Belgians have a reputation for being very gentle animals.

Belgian horses back up and turn a wagon in a team competition, to show how well trained they are.

Mules also make good work animals. A mule is a cross between a male donkey, or jack, and a mare. Draft mules are often the result of crossing a very big donkey, called a Mammoth Jack, with a draft horse mare. Mules do the same sorts of work as horses.

Three mules team up with a horse to pull a plow. If a farmer has both sorts of animals, he may combine them in this way.

Percherons pull the hay wagon, bringing food to cattle in the wintertime.

Draft horses are used on many ranches to bring hay to the cattle during the wintertime. When the grass isn't growing, the cattle need to be fed every day. When it is very wet, horses can pull a wagon though mud which would bog down a truck. And if it is snowy, horses can pull a sled loaded with hay to feed the cattle.

Other horses also help the rancher. While some ranchers ride motorcycles instead of horses, a horse provides a quieter way for the rancher to get around without scaring his cattle. The rancher checks his animals often, riding his horse through the herd to see if any animals are hurt or sick. If he wants to check on a calf, he swings a rope with a loop on the end towards the calf, catching its foot as the loop closes. Then he gets off his horse, lays the calf down, and looks it over. A good cow horse knows how to separate an animal out of the herd. It will stand still while the rancher looks at the calf and will back up to keep the rope tight so the calf can't struggle free.

While any kind of riding horse may be used to work cattle, the Quarter Horse is the most popular ranch breed. Quarter Horses are strong and muscular and tend to be gentle and reliable. Many Quarter Horses have a natural talent for working cattle and can cut one cow out of the herd with ease even if it was never trained to do so.

While a worried cow looks on, a rancher looks over her calf. The horse keeps the rope tight.

Farmers and ranchers also like to compete with their horses. In pulling contests, teams of horses compete to see which can pull the heaviest load. In team competitions, teams pull neat, shiny wagons and judges decide which horses are the best trained and most well behaved. Cow horses are also used in competitions such as calf-roping and barrel racing.

Barrel racing is a challenge for both horse and rider.

6. Other Animal Helpers

Horses aren't the only animals that help farmers and ranchers. Cats and dogs can be especially useful, too.

CATS

Most farms and ranches have barn cats that catch mice. Barns are popular places for mice to live. There is lots of hay for building nests and plenty of grain to eat. The barn cats are usually left pretty much alone to do their job of mouse hunting. The cats mate, have their kittens, and grow up in the barn and around the barnyard, without ever going into the house. While some barn cats stay away from people, others enjoy human companionship and like being petted, just like house cats.

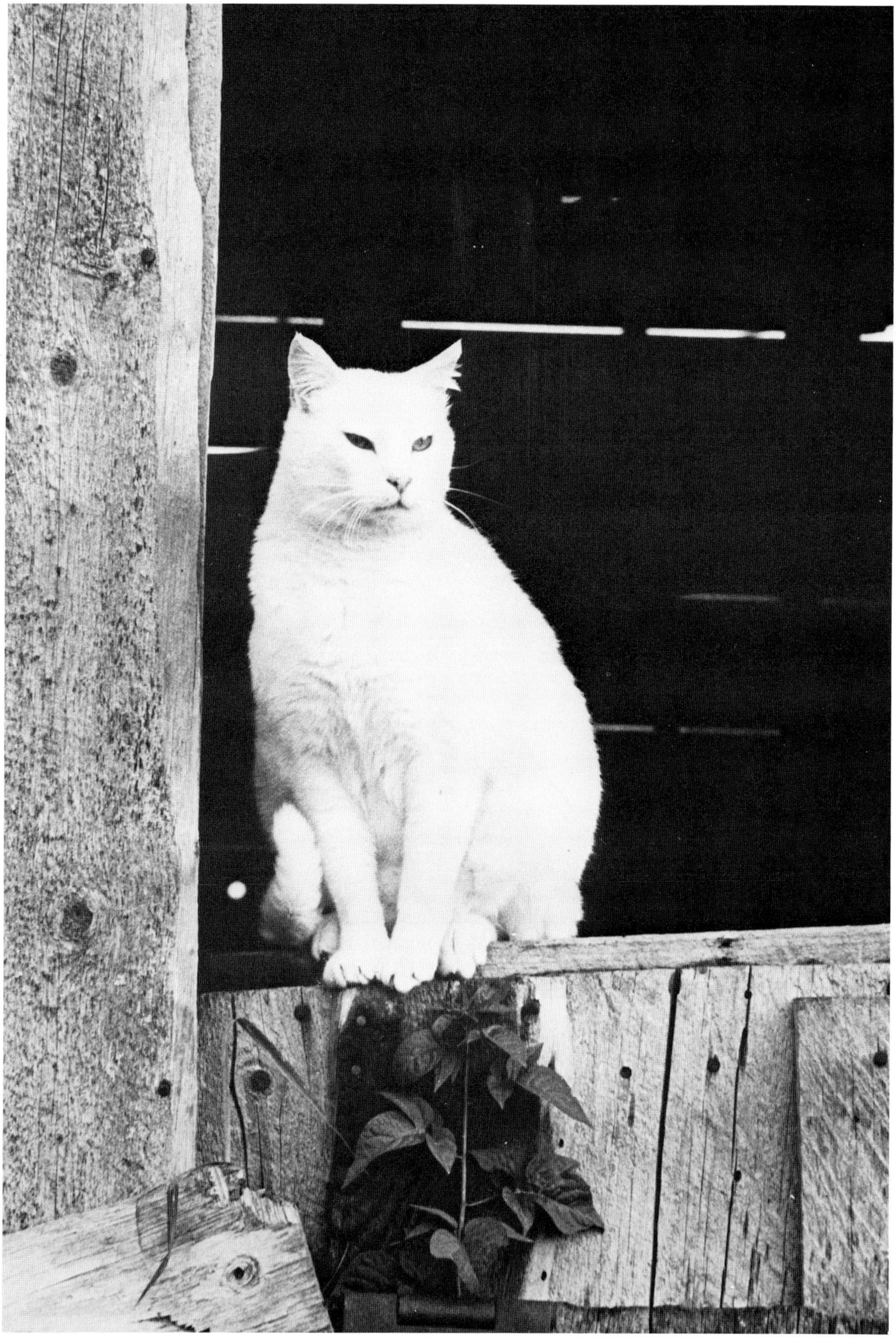

DOGS

Dogs work on ranches in many ways. Some ranch dogs capture mice, but most have a particular job of their own and are bred especially for that work. Many dog breeds started as sheepdogs. The German Shepherd, the Old English Sheepdog, and collies of various kinds were all bred originally as sheep-herding animals. Today, these breeds are mostly kept as pets. A dog called the Border Collie is probably the most popular working sheep-herding breed. Border Collies are often black and white or bluish-gray and white. They are masters at working sheep. The Border Collie knows just how to get the sheep to go where it wants them to. It will lie down tensely at one side of the flock, staring at the sheep so they avoid the dog and move past. If they begin to go in the wrong direction, the dog is on its feet in a flash, changing position so that the sheep return to the correct path. A well-trained Border Collie watches for hand signals from the shepherd which tell him where to move the sheep.

Chester is a sheepdog, a cross between two herding breeds—the Australian Shepherd and the Border Collie.

Other dogs herd cattle. Sheep-herding breeds can be used with cattle, but special cattle-herding breeds also exist. These animals, such as the Blue Heeler and Australian Cattle Dog, are small dogs that control the cattle by nipping at their heels.

This Blue Heeler-Australian Shepherd crossbreed knows how to get a cow moving.

Other breeds of dogs are used for guarding sheep. They are very different from herding dogs. While a herding dog needs to be able to control sheep and chase them in the direction it wants them to go, a guard dog must stay with the sheep and protect them from danger. It needs to know not to chase the sheep. The Great Pyrenees from France, the Komondor from Hungary, and the Kuvasz from Hungary are all large, white dogs bred especially for guarding sheep. Other guard dogs exist in other countries, but these three breeds are the most common in America.

A guard dog is put with the sheep from the time it is a puppy. It is fed out in the pasture and not allowed near the house. The dog and the sheep get used to one another as companions. A good guard dog is at home with its woolly friends and prefers them to people. It chases other dogs which come near the sheep and keeps coyotes away. A good guard dog can be annoying to its owners when they work with the flock, since the dog may try to keep them away from the sheep.

Maggie, a Kuvasz, stands guard over her flock.

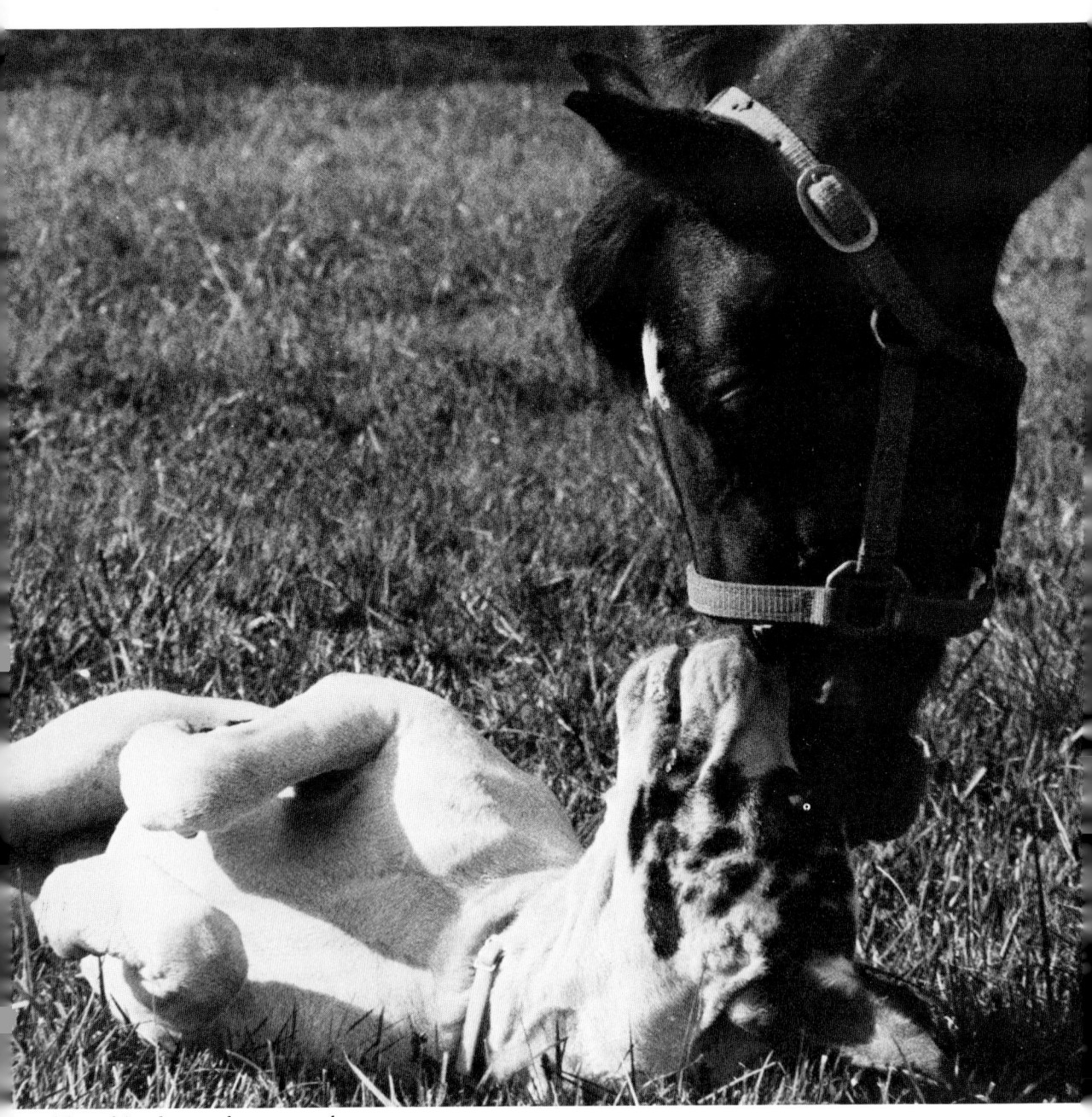

Two friends nuzzle one another.

Without domesticated animals, we would have a hard time. We would have to hunt for our meat, and we would have only an occasional wild egg to eat and no milk to drink. Our modern farms could not have developed without the help of strong draft animals, and large flocks and herds of animals couldn't have been kept without herd and guard dogs. Besides benefiting our diet and easing our work, these animals provide companionship for us and for one another.

Index

African geese, 53
Alpine goats, 21, 23, 24
Angora goat, 25
Angus cattle, 26, 29, 30
Araucana chicken, 45
Australian Cattle Dog, 72
Australian Shepherd, 71, 73
Ayrshire cows, 18

beef cattle, 9, 27–30, 63, 64, 65; breeds of, 29–30
Belgian horses, 60, 61
billy goats, 22
Blue Heeler, 72, 73
boar pigs, 35
Border Collie, 70, 71
Brahman cattle, 30
branding, 28
Brown Swiss cows, 13, 18
bulls, 14, 28, 30
butter, 19

calves, 13–14, 26, 27–28, 30, 64, 65
camels, 12
cats, 9, 68, 69
Charolais cattle, 30, 31
chickens, 8, 9, 44–48; for eggs, 9, 44–47; for meat, 9, 48
chicks, 43, 44, 46
Clydesdale horses, 60
Columbia sheep, 41
coyotes, 74
cream, 19, 20

dairy cows, 9, 12–19, 22, 27, 30; breeds of, 16–18; milking of, 14–16, 73
dogs, 9, 10, 70–74, 76; guard breeds, 74, 77; herding breeds, 70–72, 74–76
domesticated animals, 8–10, 75
Domesticated Mallard, 50, 51
donkey, 10, 61, 62
down feathers, 52
ducks, 49–51
Duroc hogs, 36

eggs, 43, 44–46, 47, 48, 76; chicken, colors, of, 45; chicken, numbers laid, 45; duck, 50, 51
Emden geese, 54
European goats, 24
ewe, 40–42

farm, 7
feedlot, 28
fleece, 42
foal, 59

gander, 52
geese, 49, 52–54
German shepherd, 70
goats, 9, 11, 12, 20–25, 39
goslings, 54
Great Pyrenees dog, 74
guard animals, 10, 52, 53, 74, 75
Guernsey cows, 18
guinea hens, 55

Hampshire pigs, 36, 37
heart valves, 38
heifers, 28, 30
Hereford cattle, 29, 65
Holstein cows, 16, 17, 19
horns, 21
horses, 9, 10, 59, 66, 76; breeds of, 60; cow, 64, 65, 66; draft, 59, 60–63, 66

Jersey cows, 16, 17, 19

kids, 12, 21, 22, 23
Komondor dog, 74
Kuvasz dog, 74, 75

lambs, 6, 39, 40–42, 75
lard, 38
leather, 38
Limousin cattle, 30
llamas, 10, 11
Longhorn cattle, 30

Mammoth Jack donkey, 62
mare, 59
meat, 7, 9, 14, 27, 30, 35, 39, 43, 48, 50, 52, 55, 56
milk, 12, 14–19, 20, 30, 35; amount of, 16, 19, 20; color of, 19; richness of, 19
mohair, 25
mules, 62
Muscovy duck, 49

nanny goats, 21–22
Nubian goats, 20, 21, 23, 25

Old English Sheepdog, 70
oxen, 59

Pekin ducks, 50
Percheron horses, 58, 60, 63
piglets, 34, 35
pigs, 9, 32–38; as pets, 33; breeds of, 36; mudbaths, 37; uses of, 38
poultry, 43–57
pulling contests, 66
pygmy goat, 24

Quarter Horse, 64, 65, 67

ranch, 8
Red Jungle Fowl, 8
rooster, 47
Rouen ducks, 50, 51

Santa Gertrudis cattle, 30
shearing sheep, 42
sheep, 6, 9, 10, 39–42, 74, 75; breeds of, 39
Shorthorn cattle, 30
Simmenthal cattle, 30
Southdown sheep, 39
sow pigs, 35
steers, 28
Suffolk sheep, 39

testes, 28
tractor, 59
Toulouse geese, 54
turkeys, 56–57; breeds of, 57; wild, 57

Yorkshire pigs, 36

waterfowl, 49, 54
wool, 39, 42

```
636
.PAT    Patent
          Farm animals
```

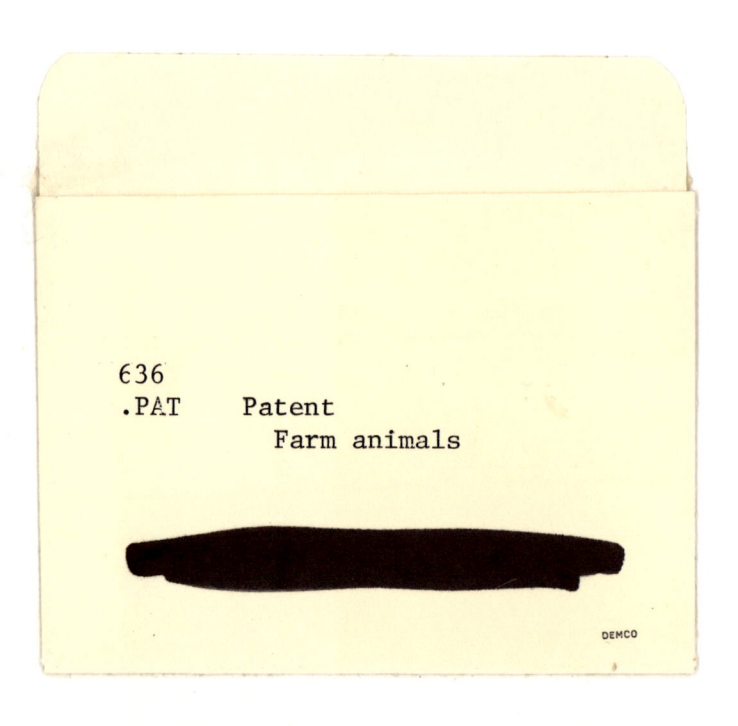